Phillis Sings Out Freedom

The Story of George Washington and Phillis Wheatley

Ann Malaspina   Illustrated by **Susan Keeter**

Albert Whitman & Company
Chicago, Illinois

AUTUMN, 1775

Sitting high on his horse, General George Washington looked out at his soldiers, gathered on a field in Cambridge, Massachusetts.

Some of the men were too young to be soldiers. Others were too old. Their coats were tattered and their powder bags were empty.

The war had begun. Could his ragged Continental Army lead a revolution against the king of England and the mighty British Empire?

Across the Charles River in Boston,
the British army was trapped, surrounded
by General Washington's soldiers. They couldn't
escape from Boston, except by sea.

Every day, the well-trained soldiers marched down
the streets in bright red uniforms and shiny black boots.
They built forts on the hills, preparing for General Washington
to attack. They were ready.

As golden autumn leaves fell along the river, General Washington taught his soldiers to take orders and aim their muskets. He broke up fights and showed the men how to work together. Slowly, the soldiers became an army.

General Washington still needed more powder for the cannons, and more cannons to go to battle. His soldiers needed new muskets, but he had no money for cannons and muskets.

General Washington feared he might not win this revolution!

Miles away, in a house in Providence, Rhode Island, Phillis Wheatley held her quill pen above the pot of ink. She had fled Boston, where King George III's soldiers marched.

On the desk, the candle flame wavered, like her thoughts on the war. She had many British friends. They had helped her to become a famous poet. In Boston, the colonists spoke of liberty, but some still owned slaves.

Still, her heart lay with the colonists. In a poem, Phillis wrote that British tyranny enslaved the land. Colonists had to pay the king's taxes, but they could not vote for the Parliament that set the taxes. America must win this war!

After all, Phillis knew about freedom—and how it felt to live in chains. Closing her eyes, she thought of Africa, where she was born.

She saw her mother in a small village, worshipping the sun at dawn. That was her only memory before the slave traders came, carrying casks of rum. How many casks to buy a young girl? Not many at all.

Then the slave ship snatched her away across the wide ocean.

On a summer day, she was led off the ship to a Boston wharf.
Wrapped in dirty carpet, she waited to be sold like a sack of sugar.

At the slave auction, the strong men were bought first. "What's the price of the small girl?" asked a woman in fine clothes.

Just a "trifle," the slave trader said. Not much at all.

The slave trader took the money, and the woman took the girl.

At their mansion on King Street, Susanna Wheatley and her husband, John, gave the little girl clothes and warm food. Their twin children, Nathaniel and Mary, had never seen a slave so thin and frail. She was so young that her front teeth were still missing! Soon the Wheatleys gave her a name—Phillis, after the ship that stole her to slavery.

Susanna grew fond of Phillis and kept her close by. She gave her young slave only light chores, like dusting the rooms and polishing the table. After Phillis served the tea to visitors, Susanna let her stay and listen—and Phillis drank up every word.

One day, Phillis began writing English letters on the wall. Everyone was surprised. Could a slave be educated?

Mary taught Phillis to read—not just English, but Latin, too. She read the Bible and Greek myths. She studied history and geography—and poems, line by line.

Phillis loved words—loud words, like "mighty" and "thundering," and bright words, like "sparkling" and "radiant."

Soon, she was writing poetry.

Phillis's poems were about many things—heroes, hurricanes, God, the ocean, Africa, and freedom.

People read Phillis's poems in newspapers, but not everyone thought a slave girl could write those soaring words. No printer in Boston would publish her book of poems.

In 1772, Phillis stood before eighteen of Boston's most important men. Even the governor of the Massachusetts Colony was there. Phillis had to prove she was a poet.

Her heart beating hard, she answered the men's questions.

Finally, they agreed. "WE whose Names are underwritten, do assure the World, that the POEMS . . . were . . . written by Phillis," they wrote, signing their names one by one.

The next year, her book, *Poems on Various Subjects, Religious and Moral,* was published in England.

And Mr. Wheatley set Phillis free.

No longer a slave, Phillis wanted to help free the colonists. But all she had was her pen.
Maybe she could write a poem—a poem for General Washington.
She dipped her pen in the black ink and wrote the date, October 26, 1775.

In December 1775, Phillis's letter and poem reached General Washington. He had heard of the famous slave poet.

General Washington put on his spectacles and began to read. Phillis's rhymes made the poem sing!

> *Proceed, great chief, with virtue on thy side,*
> *Thy ev'ry action let the goddess guide.*
> *A crown, a mansion, and a throne that shine,*
> *With gold unfading, WASHINGTON! be thine.*

General Washington was flattered by her praise, though he wanted to be a great general, not a king. Still, his army wasn't strong enough to defeat the British. What if Phillis Wheatley was wrong about him?

Winter gales blew, and the Charles River turned to ice. The wind tore through the soldiers' coats, and snow piled on their huts and tents at night.

General Washington sent a fleet to block ships bringing supplies to the British. The redcoats tore down houses and chopped trees for fuel. They were hungry and cold, just like the colonial troops.

When Christmas arrived, hundreds of General Washington's men vanished. Tired of being soldiers, they had gone home to their families—leaving his army weaker than ever. Washington was growing more worried every day.

Then, as the old year ended, General Washington saw new reason for hope. An officer named Henry Knox had hatched a daring plan. He and his brother rode horses three hundred miles to Fort Ticonderoga in New York, a British fort captured by the colonists. The fort was full of cannons.

Knox and his brother loaded the cannons on barges to cross Lake George. Through snowy forests and across the frozen Hudson River, the men traveled back.

On New Year's Day, more men arrived to join Washington's troops. Three weeks later, Knox and his men returned, with sixty tons of cannons and other guns for the Continental Army.

General Washington had not forgotten Phillis Wheatley's poem. She believed that he was a great leader.

In February 1776, he sent her a letter.

"Dear Miss Wheatley," wrote General Washington. " . . . Thank you most sincerely for your polite notice of me, in the elegant Lines you enclosed." He praised her "great poetical Talents." He called her a genius! He even invited her to visit him.

Spring was almost here, and the Continental Army was finally ready to battle the British.

On the night of March 4, 1776, General Washington's men dragged the cannons up the hills above Boston and aimed them at the city below. They painted logs to look like more cannons and built barricades with branches and dirt.

When the sun rose, the British in Boston saw the cannon barrels and the soldiers way up on the hills. The redcoats were astonished at the weapons and the many troops. Their guns couldn't reach General Washington and his mighty Continental Army!

Days later, the British army retreated and sailed north, leaving Boston to the American colonists.

The Continental Army had won its first victory.

And with her poems,
Phillis Wheatley sang out
freedom—for herself and
a new nation.

In his letter, George Washington invited Phillis Wheatley to meet him at his headquarters in Cambridge in 1776. It would have been a strange sight—the tall general with an army to lead and the small former slave woman with only a pen. If they did meet, no one knows what they said to each other. The war soon took them in different directions.

For eight long years, George Washington served as commander-in-chief of the Continental Army in the Revolutionary War. He lost more battles than he won, but he won important battles, too. His army finally defeated the British at Yorktown, Virginia, in October 1781. The peace treaty recognizing American independence was signed in 1783. The American colonies were free, and a new nation was born. On April 30, 1789, Washington became the first president of the United States.

Phillis Wheatley had her own battles to fight. Freed from slavery in 1773, she needed to earn a living. She tried to sell her poems, but during the war people saved their money for food and clothing. Desperately poor, she worked in a hotel. Wheatley married a free black man named John Peters. His grocery business failed. They had two children who died. Less than a year after the war ended, Wheatley died on December 5, 1784. She was only about thirty-one. Her newborn baby did not survive, and the mother and child were buried in an unmarked grave.

Like that of most slaves, Wheatley's life was not well documented. Many details are not known for sure. But her poems will not ever be forgotten. One of Phillis Wheatley's last poems celebrated the end of the Revolutionary War. It is titled "Liberty and Peace."

In his will, Washington wrote that all his slaves were to be freed after his wife, Martha's, death. He died on December 14, 1799.

This is the document that the men signed in Boston in 1772:

WE whose Names are underwritten, do assure the World, that the POEMS specified in the following Page were (as we verily believe) written by Phillis, a young Negro Girl, who was but a few Years since, brought an uncultivated Barbarian from Africa, and has ever since been, and now is, under the Disadvantage of serving as a Slave in a Family in this Town. She has been examined by some of the best Judges, and is thought qualified to write them.

FURTHER READING

Clinton, Catherine. *Phillis's Big Test.* New York: Houghton Mifflin Books for Children, 2008.

Giblin, James Cross. *George Washington: A Picture Book Biography.* New York: Scholastic, 1998.

Lasky, Kathryn. *A Voice of Her Own: A Story of Phillis Wheatley, Slave Poet.* Cambridge, Mass.: Candlewick Press, 2005.

Maestro, Betsy. *Liberty or Death: The American Revolution 1763-1783.* New York: HarperCollins, 2005.

Miller, Brandon Marie. *George Washington for Kids: His Life and Times. 21 Activities.* Chicago: Chicago Review Press, 2007.

Thomas, Peggy. *Farmer George Plants a Nation.* Honesdale, Pa.: Boyds Mill Press, 2008.

For my grandmother, Mabel B. Gould, who loved words.—A.M.

To my daughters, Sara Christine Tucker and Emma Rose Tucker.—S.K.

Library of Congress Cataloging-in-Publication Data

Malaspina, Ann, 1957-
Phillis sings out freedom : the story of George Washington and Phillis Wheatley / Ann Malaspina ; illustrated by Susan Keeter.
p. cm.
ISBN 978-0-8075-6545-2
1. Washington, George, 1732-1799—Military leadership—Miscellanea—Juvenile literature. 2. United States. Continental Army—History—Miscellanea—Juvenile literature. 3. Wheatley, Phillis, 1753-1784—Miscellanea—Juvenile literature.
4. Poets, American—Colonial period, ca. 1600-1775—Miscellanea—Juvenile literature. I. Keeter, Susan, ill. II. Title.
E312.25.M35 2010 973.4'1092—dc22 2009049286

Text copyright © 2010 by Ann Malaspina. Illustrations copyright © 2010 by Susan Keeter.
Published in 2010 by Albert Whitman & Company.

Printed in China.
10 9 8 7 6 5 4 3 2 1 HH 15 14 13 12 11 10

The illustrations are rendered in oil paint on gessoed paper.
The design is by Carol Gildar.

For more information about Albert Whitman & Company, please visit our web site at www.albertwhitman.com.